GEORGE W. BUSH

OTHER BOOKS BY LOUANN ATKINS TEMPLE IN THE BIOGRAPHY FOR BEGINNING HISTORIANS SERIES

Barbara Bush

Laura Bush

Lyndon B. Johnson

George H. W. Bush

Lady Bird Johnson

GEORGE W. BUSH

A Biography for Beginning Historians

LOUANN ATKINS TEMPLE

THE LBJ FOUNDATION
BRISCOE CENTER
FOR AMERICAN HISTORY
Distributed by the University of Texas Press

First edition, 2025

Requests for permission to reproduce material from this work should be sent to permissions@utpress.utexas.edu.

♾ The paper used in this book meets the minimum requirements of ANSI/NISO Z39.48-1992 (R1997) (Permanence of Paper).

Library of Congress Cataloging-in-Publication Data

Names: Temple, Louann Atkins author
Title: George W. Bush : a biography for beginning historians / Louann Atkins Temple.
Description: First edition. | [Austin] : The LBJ Foundation and Briscoe Center for American History, 2025. | Includes bibliographical references. | Audience: Ages 8–12 | Audience: Grades 4–6
Identifiers: LCCN 2025016646 (print) | LCCN 2025016647 (ebook)
ISBN 978-1-4773-3208-5 paperback
ISBN 978-1-4773-3209-2 pdf
ISBN 978-14773-3210-8 epub
Subjects: LCSH: Bush, George W. (George Walker), 1946– | Juvenile literature | Bush, George W. (George Walker), 1946– | Family—Juvenile literature | Presidents—United States—Biography—Juvenile literature | Governors—Texas—Biography—Juvenile literature | Children of presidents—United States—Biography | United States—Politics and government—Juvenile literature | LCGFT: Biographies
Classification: LCC E903 .T46 2025 (print) | LCC E903 (ebook) | DDC 973.931092 $a B—dc23/eng/20250521
LC record available at https://lccn.loc.gov/2025016646
LC ebook record available at https://lccn.loc.gov/2025016647

doi:10.7560/332085

To Uncle Frank
who taught me to love history

When I entered politics, I made a decision:
I would confront problems, not pass them on
to future generations. . . . As I told my advisers,
"I didn't take this job to play small ball."

—GEORGE WALKER BUSH

CONTENTS

GEORGE W. BUSH

INTRODUCTION

George Walker Bush is a more complex man than he is credited with being. His casual personality misleads people into thinking he is simple to understand. He is not.

Two necessary requirements for understanding him are learning about his family relationships and the impact of 9/11 on him.

The forty-third president of the United States has combined in himself the interests and ambitions of his father (sports, oil, politics), the personality of his mother (funny, biting, at ease with others), and his own experiences (family and national tragedies, restless moving from job to job, struggling for sobriety, religious development) to become his own man and a unique leader whom historians struggle to understand. Writers have speculated about the good and bad of George Bush's relationships with his parents and about their accomplishments versus his own, but the importance of these issues boils down to the fact that he grew up in a loving family that taught him well. He expressed it best when he said, "I've never had a fear of losing. I didn't *like* to lose. But having parents who give you unconditional love, I think it means I had the peace of mind to know that even with failure, there was love. So I never feared failure."

While president, he took on the burden of protecting his country from a second terrorist attack after 9/11 like Atlas carrying the world on his shoulders. He has said, "The story of that week is the key to understanding my presidency. . . . I could never forget what happened to America that day. I would pour my heart and soul into protecting the country, whatever it took." It took him to some unexpected and dangerous places.

CHAPTER 1

STARTING OUT IN TEXAS

George Walker Bush belongs to the Barbara and George Herbert Walker Bush family and to the state of Texas. He was shaped by both, and he proudly carries their characteristics along with his own uniqueness. Like his father, George W. pursued careers in oil and politics and loves sports. Like his mother, he is direct, bantering, and outspoken, making friends easily. He once explained, "I had my daddy's eyes and my mother's mouth," but George H. W. Bush's kind eyes and Barbara Bush's plain-speaking manner barely begin to explain these two complex people or their eldest son.

George the father worked endless hours and traveled frequently. Nevertheless, the children knew they were always free to call him on the phone whenever they wanted. Barbara kept him present in Georgie's mind by showing the boy scrapbooks she kept of his father and by talking about him affectionately. When at home, the father and son connected through sports. George coached Georgie's Little League team and took him to football games. George W. is still proud of the day he and his father were playing catch together, and his father said, "Son, you've arrived. I can throw it to you as hard as I want." His form of discipline was to say, "I am disappointed"—that was it.

Barbara Bush was super organized, a hands-on mother who spent her days reading to her children when they were small; when they were older, her days included driving them to "more Little League games than you can even imagine," as she said; being a Cub Scout den mother; supervising their study; and disciplining them firmly but without losing her temper. Her husband called her the Enforcer. She had a quick wit. She always spoke her mind, often colorfully. If a child behaved well, she would say something like, "That's using your head for more than a hat rack." She disliked phonies. She dealt with problems but never dwelled on them and just kept going. George W. called her "unflappable" when he remembered that the morning after Bill Clinton defeated her husband for reelection to the presidency, she said, "Well, now, that's behind us. It's time to move on." Her children remembered that she taught them never to brag or to act as if they thought they were important. She taught them their sense of values.

In a memoir, George W. wrote about both his parents, "Growing up, my brothers and sister and I knew that while they might not approve of everything we did (and would certainly tell us when they didn't), our mother and dad would always love us. Always. Forever. Unwaveringly. Without question. They said it and they showed it."

George the father wanted Georgie to have the same New England educational experiences he had—Andover for high school and Yale for college—and he involved him in his political campaigns and his administrative decisions after he became the forty-first president. He stepped back after George W.

became the forty-third president and watched with sympathy and understanding but not interference.

On July 6, 1946, at 7:26 a.m. in New Haven, Connecticut, George Walker Bush was born—three weeks late—to East Coast parents, and his father was a student at Yale. When Georgie was two, his parents set out on their adventure to be independent by moving the family to Texas and becoming part of the burgeoning oil business in Midland. There Georgie grew up on the flatlands of a vast state under a big sky, in a town where no one locked their doors—surrounded by oil rigs and risk-takers—wearing cowboy boots and hanging a picture of Roy Rogers on his bedroom wall. High school football reigned on Friday night, and Sunday included church and backyard cookouts with the neighbors and playing catch with his father or marbles or yo-yos with his friends. Throughout his life, George emphasized that he was a rural West Texan who went to public schools: he was not a Dallas city boy or a private-school Easterner.

After Georgie, sister Robin was born and then brother Jeb. Tragedy struck early in Georgie's life when Robin, age three, was diagnosed with fatal leukemia. Their parents moved her to a hospital in New York where they hoped they could prolong her life. Georgie and baby Jeb remained in Midland and were cared for by their parents' friends and a nurse. Their mother stayed at the hospital in New York with Robin, and their father worked in Texas during the week and went to New York on weekends. Once during the summer, they were able to take Robin to their family's summer home in Kennebunkport, Maine, where Georgie got to see Robin, but he couldn't play with her.

Robin died seven months after the diagnosis, and her body was taken to Connecticut to be buried with her grandparents. George and Barbara Bush returned home to tell seven-year-old Georgie. They drove up to his school. Georgie thought he saw Robin in the car with them and ran to meet them. He asked where she was, and Barbara, holding Georgie in her lap, told him that Robin had died. Georgie watched his parents weep continuously on the drive home. He remembered that he was stunned. "I knew that Robin had been sick, but death was hard for me to imagine. Minutes before, I had had a little sister, and now, suddenly, I did not. . . . Those minutes remain the starkest memory of my childhood, a sharp pain in the midst of an otherwise happy blur. . . . I guess I learned in a harsh way, at a very early age, never to take life for granted."

Barbara said later that for a long time Georgie did not forgive them for keeping the truth from him. Whenever he had asked about Robin, they had told him that she was sick but would be better. "We thought he was too young to know," said Barbara. "But how do you tell a six-year-old, 'Your sister is going to die'?"

Over the next months, Barbara drew Georgie close to her. He, in turn, became protective of his mother. When she realized that he was spending time with her rather than with his friends because he worried about her, she began to look for ways to heal and send him back into a child's world of playing and learning.

The next years—until he was a teenager—his personality began to define itself. A tendency to be a cutup at home followed him to school, where the principal feared clownishness in him. Georgie was sent to the principal's office for disrupting a music class by painting a mustache on his face. Instead of being apologetic, the principal told Barbara, "he swaggered in as though he had been the most wonderful thing in the world." The principal swatted Georgie on his backside with a board, which was punishment that didn't bruise or hurt him and was not unusual for the time. After hearing the story, Barbara, who had arrived angry with the principal, left agreeing with him. "You don't want the class clown," she said, "you want a kid who's going to do his best." Another way Georgie and his mother were alike: When she was growing up, Barbara, too, had been known as the class clown.

In 1959, when Georgie was thirteen, the family, which now included brothers Neil and Marvin, moved to Houston, where these younger brothers spent their formative years. Soon, sister Dorothy (Doro) arrived.

Georgie spent two years at a Houston private school and then followed in his father's footsteps by attending an all-male boarding school, Phillips Academy, in Andover, Massachusetts. He called going to Andover "the hardest thing I did in my life, until I ran for president." His parents had to persuade him to stay when he called and asked to come home because he felt alone and isolated. He made Andover bearable and finally desirable by making friends, acting cocky and still clownish, and becoming a cheerleader. Here he learned to love history, and here he learned about himself that "I could make friends, and make my way, no matter where I found myself in life."

Another West Texan, Laura Welch, had been born in Midland the same year as George: 1946. She was the only child of Harold and Jenna Welch. Harold was a real estate developer, and Jenna did the bookkeeping for their business.

Laura's great loves from childhood were reading and teaching. As a child, she played at being a teacher by showing her dolls how to read. Her love turned into a career. After getting a bachelor of science in education at Southern Methodist University, she went to the University of Texas at Austin for a master's degree in library science. She served as an elementary school teacher and as a librarian in Dallas, Houston, and Austin. She and George would meet when they were both around thirty years old.

CHAPTER 2

COLLEGE AND ADULTHOOD

Again George followed family tradition when he went to Yale for college, the alma mater of his great-grandfather, his grandfather, his father, and numerous uncles and cousins. He majored in history. Here, again, he looked to friendships and fun for his satisfaction.

At this time, his father was becoming a national figure in politics. George found that many college classmates had opposing political views to those of his father's and were open about expressing their criticism without regard for his feelings.

George graduated and drifted through various jobs, helped out with multiple political campaigns, considered law school, thought about running for the Texas legislature, and finally applied and was accepted to Harvard Business School. Determined to make this choice and this accomplishment his own, he did not tell his family until after he was accepted.

He entered Harvard in 1973, graduated two years later, and headed back to Texas, to Midland, to start a career, as his father had, in the oil business. He began working for a company as a landman—one who negotiates with landowners to acquire leases, finding promising oil-drilling sites, and

Left to right: Jeb, Marvin, George H. W., Doro, Barbara, Neil, and twenty-one-year-old George W. Bush at the United States Capitol, Washington, DC, 1967. Courtesy of George H. W. Bush Presidential Library and Museum.

negotiating deals to lease them. Later he created his own company that he called Arbusto Energy, a name that was derived from the Spanish word for "bush."

At a backyard barbecue, George met his future wife, Laura Welch. It was love at first sight, remembered Laura. He asked her to play miniature golf the next night, and three months later, they married—November 5, 1977—at the First Methodist Church in Midland. Laura met most of her big new family at the wedding. George described the couple's differences and their compatibility. "Laura is calm; I am energetic. She is restful; I am restless. She is patient; I am impatient. . . . We share the same basic values. We share a West Texas upbringing that taught us that each individual is equal and equally important, but also that each individual has a responsibility to be a good neighbor and a good citizen. We both love to read, we both love spending time with our friends, and we both, very quickly, fell in love with each other."

They honeymooned on the island of Cozumel, in the Caribbean Sea off the coast of Mexico, where they toured the island full of iguanas, tanned on the beach, and played gin rummy.

Ten days before his wedding, George had announced his candidacy for US Congress. He and Laura returned from their honeymoon to hit the campaign trail, traveling across West Texas in George's Oldsmobile, with long driving hours between towns when they could just talk. In 1978, George became the Republican candidate by winning the Republican primary but lost in the general election to his Democratic opponent. In the process, a friend reported that George "loved it and he was having a great time. . . . He was such a good speaker."

The Bush family (*left to right:* Jenna, George, Laura and Barbara), Kennebunkport, Maine, August 1990. Courtesy of George H. W. Bush Presidential Library and Museum.

In 1981, Laura and George's twins, Jenna and Barbara, were born, named after their grandmothers. Laura said that she especially liked that the girls had each other because, as an only child, she had always wanted a sister.

While the twins were babies, George, searching as he always was in all areas of his life, joined the Methodist Church and began Bible study.

With this full life, he continued to play as hard as he worked, which included drinking. On his fortieth birthday, he celebrated with Laura and friends in Colorado Springs, woke up the next morning with a hangover, and struggled to do his usual three-mile daily run. Later, he remembered, "I knew I could count on the grace of God to help me change. It would not be easy, but by the end of the run, I had made up my mind: I was done drinking." It was not easy, but he succeeded.

In 1988, after serving two terms as vice president under President Ronald Reagan, George's father ran for the presidency. George moved to Washington to help run his father's campaign. As a part of the election team, he became a strength to his father, who had always been strong for him, while learning a lot about politics. His father won the presidency.

The restlessness returned, and soon George made a big move to Dallas, where he organized investors to purchase the Texas Rangers baseball team, which he managed for five years. He attended the games he so loved, sitting behind the home-team dugout next to first base, and staying to the end of every game. He got to be his gregarious self, traveling the state to promote the team with Rotary Clubs and chambers of commerce. He got to oversee the building of a new stadium and become wealthy while still keeping a quiet hand in his father's administration. Then, in 1992, his father lost his bid for reelection to Bill Clinton, mainly because of an economic recession. "Watching a good man lose made 1992 one of the worst years of my life," George wrote.

CHAPTER 3

GOVERNOR OF TEXAS AND RUNNING FOR PRESIDENT

In 1994, George once again moved on. He ran for governor of Texas against popular incumbent Ann Richards, something he had been considering for several years. By then, he knew politics from watching and helping his father, working in others' campaigns, and running for Congress himself.

Karl Rove, who had worked as a strategist for him in his congressional run, once again worked for him. Though he was proud of his father, George appeared in public as his own man.

He emphasized education reform as an issue. The public schools, at that time, were funded locally but governed by the state. George thought that formula was backward. Schools should be financed by the state so that all of them had equal amounts to spend. They should be run by their local school boards, who knew best what their particular schools needed.

He did not respond to Governor Richards' taunts when she referred to him as "Shrub," and he never publicly criticized her. He courted conservatives and evangelical Christians.

One incident during the campaign could have spoiled

his chances of winning, but he handled it by running into it headlong and thus minimizing its impact. On the opening day of dove season, George went hunting accompanied by the media. He shot a dove while the cameras clicked. Later, he discovered that he had not killed a dove at all but, rather, a songbird called a killdeer. The press might or might not find out. Bush chose to go to the local justice of the peace, tell them what he had done, and pay a fine. He announced to the press, "I have a confession to make; I am a killdeer killer. . . . Thank goodness it was not deer season; I might have shot a cow." The incident may have actually helped him by showing that he could make a mistake, apologize, and laugh at himself.

When he won the election with 53 percent of the vote, the *New York Times* called it "a stunning upset." The day of his inauguration, he received a letter from his father, which said, "You are ready for this huge challenge. You'll do just fine. You'll be a strong, honest, caring Governor." And then he was sworn in, with his hand on the Bible.

At the same time, his brother Jeb ran for governor of Florida and was defeated. Now George W. Bush was the only active politician in the family.

Bush remained governor for six years, winning a second term in 1998 by almost 70 percent of the vote. (Jeb was elected governor of Florida that same day.) He achieved much of his success by his willingness to work with both parties. In an inspired move, shortly before the 1994 election, he visited the crusty, powerful Democratic Lieutenant Governor Bob Bullock at Bullock's home. In a meeting that lasted an hour and a half, he told Bullock that he thought he was going to win, and wanted the two of them to work together. And until

Texas Governor Bush talks with former President Ford at the LBJ Presidential Library and Museum, Austin, Texas, February 1997. Courtesy of the LBJ Presidential Library and Museum.

Bullock's death in 1999, they did. Bullock was explosive, and they clashed, and then they cooperated. What they shared was an eagerness to get things done.

About Bullock, Bush said, "We had a good chemistry from the start." Democrat Bullock, in turn, endorsed Bush for both reelection as governor and election as president, saying that he had worked with governors over forty-two years and had never found one "more responsive, more dedicated, more intelligent, more inclusive."

It was not only the lieutenant governor whom Bush befriended. In the Democrat-controlled House and Senate, he dropped by to chat with both Democrats and Republicans. He called them by friendly nicknames. He invited them to breakfast at the Governor's Mansion. He refused to campaign for any Republican running against a Democratic legislator who was already in office. Much of his policy as governor focused on public education from grade school through college, just as he promised he would do. He signed bills requiring tests for elementary school students in reading and other basic skills and required Texas public colleges and universities to accept any student who graduated in the top 10 percent of their high school class.

In June 1999, Bush announced his candidacy for president from the floor of the Texas House Chamber.

Running for president was a big, ambitious step. But Bush thought he was ready. Karl Rove, Bush's close political strategist who had worked with him on previous campaigns, thought so too. Bush knew politics. He had run for state office and lost; he had run for state office and won. He had worked actively in his father's campaigns, been one of his father's political advisers, and observed his father's and his brother Jeb's careers from a close perspective.

Rove began orchestrating the process of telling the nation about Bush. Bush's impressive reelection as governor with large numbers of votes from Latinos, women, and independents convinced many Republicans of Bush's suitability for the office of the president. Rove's impressive fundraising convinced others.

Senator John McCain of Arizona, a military hero, proved to be Bush's only serious challenger. In the Republican primaries, Bush won Iowa and McCain won New Hampshire. Bush next won South Carolina and nine of thirteen more states. McCain withdrew from the race when it became apparent that Bush would win enough delegates to earn the nomination.

Bush asked Dick Cheney, who had served as his father's secretary of defense, to head a search committee for his vice president. Soon, however, Bush realized that he wanted Cheney himself because of his long government experience. Cheney had worked for two presidents, including Bush's father, and had been a leader in Congress. He could bring only three electoral votes from Wyoming, and he had health problems, but he knew the inner workings of government, and that is what Bush was looking for.

In accepting the nomination at the Republican Convention, Bush displayed the restless eagerness that propelled him. "Tonight in this hall," he said, "we resolve to be the party not of repose but of reform. We will write not footnotes but chapters in the American story. . . . Give me the opportunity to lead this nation, and I will lead."

In the same speech, he reminded people that he planned to lead with his particular brand of gusto when he said, "People say I swagger, but in Texas it's called walking."

In the general election, Bush and Cheney faced incumbent Vice President Al Gore, who had easily won the Democratic nomination, and his running mate, Senator Joe Lieberman.

On Election Day, the media announced the contest as too close to call. To be elected, a candidate must win 270 electoral votes. The election came down to the state of Florida, whose twenty-five electoral votes would have put either candidate over the top. The polls closed at 7 p.m. Beginning about

8 p.m., even though few votes had actually been counted, a number of television stations announced that Gore had won Florida. They based this judgment on interviews with voters as they left the polls and on their own statistics produced by computer programs.

Democrats celebrated. Republicans complained. Then, as results continued to come in, the media said the race was too close to call. Gore awaited more results at his home in Nashville, Tennessee, and Bush in the Governor's Mansion in Austin.

At 2 a.m., television stations named Bush the winner. Gore telephoned Bush and congratulated him. He asked Bush to give him time to tell his supporters, then he would call Bush back.

Gore left his hotel and headed to a rally where he planned to concede the election. Seconds before he went onstage, his staff intercepted him to say that Bush's lead was shrinking as votes continued to come in and that he should wait for more results.

Gore telephoned Bush again, and with the sound of his supporters chanting his name in the background, he said, "Governor, as you know, the results are very close, and I think it would be irresponsible of me to concede, so I'm going to have to withdraw the concession I made to you before."

Bush, sitting with Laura and his parents and brother Jeb, was taken aback. He thought he had been elected president, and now his opponent was saying, "No." His response, as he admitted later, was "abrupt."

Whatever Bush's response to Gore, those with Gore heard him say to Bush, "You don't have to be snippy about it."

On that unfriendly note, the two sides waited. At 5 a.m.,

Florida announced that the law demanded an automatic recount because the numbers were so close. The Bushes, the Gores, and the country continued to wait—for thirty-six days—while recounts continued and both sides tried to gain an advantage through court suits. On December 12, a United States Supreme Court ruling recognized the results of the Florida election in Bush's favor, giving Bush enough Electoral College votes to make him the next president of the United States—271 versus Gore's 266—even though Gore had won the popular vote nationwide by just under a percentage point.

CHAPTER 4

INAUGURATION AND FIRST MONTHS AS PRESIDENT

Bush's inauguration was the first of the twenty-first century. It began at noon on January 20 on a cold, rainy day. Many on the inaugural platform draped themselves in clear plastic raincoats, but Laura stood uncovered in a bright blue coat and matching dress. The new president, in a dark suit and a soft blue tie, wore an overcoat midway through the chilly service. After taking the oath of office and kissing Laura and Jenna and Barbara, all standing beside him, he walked back to his parents' seats to greet them as the new president of the United States.

He began his inaugural address by thanking Gore for "a contest conducted with spirit and ended in grace." His soothing speech emphasized certain words repeatedly: *civility, courage, compassion, children, community.* He paid honor to immigrants; he stated that "no insignificant person was ever born." He made biblical references. During the ceremony, camera operators repeatedly wiped rain off their lenses to erase a foggy picture.

The ceremony was followed by a drive down Pennsylvania Avenue. Rain continued while they huddled under umbrellas to watch the parade. In front of the White House, military service members on horseback, high school and college marching bands from across the country, and floats with patriotic themes honored the new president and his wife for an hour and a half.

As soon as he got to the White House, speculation began about how much he would involve his father in his decisions. In actuality, it was not much. Bush's father, called Bush 41 due to the fact that he had been the forty-first president, saw his role not as an adviser but as a lightener of the heavy load carried by his son, called Bush 43 as the forty-third president. Bush 41 sometimes sent him e-mails containing corny jokes. As Bush 43 said, "His humor was often just what I needed."

The new president kept a disciplined and strenuous schedule that began in the Oval Office at seven each morning. He was punctual and demanded the same of his staff. Along with meetings and briefings and problem-solving, he always managed to get in at least an hour of exercise, and he found time for extensive reading, which over the course of his presidency included fourteen biographies of his hero Abraham Lincoln and, over the course of each year, going through the Bible from beginning to end. He disliked state dinners and press briefings and avoided them when possible.

His daughters brought two happy family events during his first term. Jenna graduated from the University of Texas at Austin, her mother's alma mater. And like her father, Barbara graduated from Yale.

During his first months as president, Bush dealt with domestic issues of consequence, and he appointed the first African American secretary of state, Colin Powell, followed by

President and Mrs. Bush board *Air Force One*, June 2001. Courtesy of George W. Bush Presidential Library.

the first African American woman secretary of state, Condoleezza Rice.

Bush described himself as a "compassionate conservative," meaning that he believed in small government and in businesses competing with little interference from government.

His way of stimulating the economy was through cutting taxes, which yielded mixed results. The bad: less money for the federal government and more wealth inequality among citizens. The good: a surging stock market and declining unemployment.

He thought that faith-based groups, charities, and local organizations could help people in need more effectively than the government. For that reason, he allowed those groups to receive federal grants, which some saw as allowing religion to interfere in government.

He advocated for the No Child Left Behind Act, which

he hoped would give all children an equal education. He was appalled that on an international math test, America came in nineteenth place of the twenty-one countries tested. His plan required students to be tested in math and reading skills. The schools that failed would be given government help, but if they continued to fail, they would be penalized, and students would be allowed to change schools. Although the plan had bipartisan support, and many students were achieving higher math and reading scores than in previous years, it, too, was criticized for taking away control from states and giving it to the federal government. For every undertaking, he had both supporters and critics.

With No Child Left Behind, Bush successfully used the same ability to work with the opposing party that he had demonstrated as governor in partnership with Bob Bullock. This time his ally was the Lion of the Senate, Democrat Ted Kennedy. Kennedy was brother to President John Kennedy and Attorney General Robert Kennedy, served on the Senate education committee, and was influential throughout his party. Bush introduced No Child Left Behind during his first week in office and invited Senator Kennedy to the White House to see if they could work together. They did. He courted not just Kennedy but many other members of Congress as well. One newspaper commented that he was conducting "the biggest charm offensive of any modern chief executive."

It worked. In January of 2002, with the support of Kennedy and other lawmakers of both parties, No Child Left Behind became law in a landslide vote.

CHAPTER 5

9/11

New presidents learn from studying the presidents before them, and they learn on the job. Bush had been on the job for only eight months when America faced attacks on its homeland on September 11, 2001, a date that would become known as "9/11." However, Bush could not be taught by previous presidents how to react because no president in living memory had faced terrorist strikes on US soil. This president was on his own in dealing with unprecedented circumstances.

The attacks were devastating. Nearly three thousand Americans were killed on 9/11 when terrorists hijacked and took control of four planes. Two attacked the Twin Towers of the World Trade Center in New York, one rammed into the Pentagon in Washington, and one crashed in Pennsylvania. Those responsible for planning the attacks were not from one country but were hiding in several countries, and they could not be found. Americans had the wind knocked out of them.

Prior to the attacks, 9/11 had begun pleasantly for President Bush. He was in Sarasota, Florida, where he intended to highlight his plans for education reform by visiting a classroom at Emma E. Booker Elementary School. He jogged before daylight, read the Bible, and had a light breakfast. Then,

President Bush gets a security briefing by phone as a White House aide points to television coverage showing a second attack on the World Trade Center, Sarasota, Florida, September 2001. Courtesy of George W. Bush Presidential Library.

on the way to the event, he puzzled over a message from Secretary of State Condoleezza Rice, telling him that a commercial airliner had struck the World Trade Center in New York. That didn't seem possible—unless, perhaps, the pilot had had a heart attack.

Later, as Bush sat in a classroom talking to students and their teacher, chief of staff Andy Card entered the room while the children were reading and whispered to him, "A second plane hit the second tower. America is under attack."

Bush's outrage at the news as he looked at the innocent children and his determination to be strong for the country's sake—as he noticed reporters in the back of the room—kept him calmly continuing the lesson until it ended seven minutes later. He would get the facts, he thought, and then speak to the country.

He raced to a holding room, watched the TV coverage of the unfolding catastrophe, wrote out his comments, and went up to a microphone, where the audience of parents, teachers, and members of the community expected him to talk about education. "Ladies and gentlemen," he said, "this is a difficult moment for America. . . . Two airplanes have crashed into the World Trade Center in an apparent terrorist attack on our country. . . . Terrorism against our nation will not stand." He ended with a prayer for the victims, then left quickly, headed for *Air Force One* under instructions from the Secret Service.

When the Bush party arrived at the airport, agents carrying assault rifles surrounded the plane. The pilots had two of the four engines already running. Bomb-detecting dogs sniffed the passengers and luggage as they boarded. The military, the Secret Service, and the presidential staff took charge, escorting the president to a private compartment and instructing the press and congressmen traveling with them to make no telephone calls. The plane rose quickly to thirty thousand feet. When another plane was seen in the area, *Air Force One* changed course to be sure they were not being followed. They were not.

Immediately Bush insisted that he be taken to Washington. The Secret Service members refused due to concerns that more attacks would occur. Bush angrily argued with them, and they repeatedly told him that it was not his decision to make. They had to protect him. After they heard that the Pentagon outside Washington had been struck, they were even more certain he should not return.

In order to get fuel, reduce the number of passengers on board, and add some food, the plane landed at Barksdale Air Force Base, near Shreveport, Louisiana, where bombers lined the taxiway awaiting them. There, nonessential passengers were left behind; a fourteen-hour supply of fuel was pumped into the gas tanks; and forty gallons of coffee, seventy box lunches, and twenty-five pounds of bananas were added to the plane's supplies. Again the presidential party took off, this time climbing to eight miles above land escorted by three F-16 fighters. By then, all planes throughout the country had been grounded. These were the only four airplanes over American skies.

Bush soon learned that a fourth commercial plane, which had been under the control of terrorists, had crashed in Pennsylvania. After calling family members to tell them goodbye, a group of brave passengers revolted against the terrorists but could not regain control of the airplane. Had the terrorists intended to use the plane to attack the Capitol? The White House?

Air Force One left Barksdale Air Force Base and headed for Offutt Air Force Base in Nebraska. It was there, in an underground bunker, that Bush learned that the terrorists were from al-Qaeda, a fundamentalist Islamic network led by Osama bin Laden, a wealthy Saudi who had been expelled from his own country. Al-Qaeda was headquartered in Afghanistan, where the Taliban government supported them. But the terrorists who hijacked the commercial airline planes had been hiding and training in America.

Bush finally got to talk to Laura and was reassured that she, Barbara, and Jenna were safe. The Secret Service had whisked Laura out of a No Child Left Behind meeting in Senator Kennedy's office. With guns pulled, they rushed her to an underground room in their own Washington headquarters. At the University of Texas at Austin, the Secret Service pounded on Jenna's dorm door and whisked her to a secure location. At Yale, in New Haven, Connecticut, Barbara was taken to a hotel on the outskirts of town.

Bush called his mother and his father, who agreed that he should return to Washington. When his mother told him that they were in a motel in Wisconsin, he said, "What in the world are you doing there?" She replied, "Son, you grounded our plane."

Finally, *Air Force One* headed for Washington and landed at Andrews Air Force Base at 6:30 p.m. During the ten-minute helicopter ride to the White House, Bush could see fires still smoldering at the Pentagon. As he came into Washington, Dick Cheney left for Camp David so that the president and vice president would not be in the same place in the event of another attack.

That night, sitting at his desk in the Oval Office, Bush addressed the nation on television, reassuring Americans in a subdued voice that the country would continue to operate as usual; that we had allies around the world; and that "our military is powerful and it's prepared."

In the following days, President Bush would speak to Americans repeatedly, the range of his own emotions clearly displayed—powerlessness to help those grieving, sadness, fear, anger, determination—evolving into a plan of action announced to a joint session of Congress.

On September 14, Bush flew to New York and stood amid the still-smoldering remains of the Twin Towers. He wore a windbreaker rather than his usual dark suit and tie. When a firefighter pulled him up on top of a burned-out fire truck so the crowd could see him, he put his arm around the man

Three days after the 9/11 attacks on the World Trade Center, President Bush rallies first responders at Ground Zero, New York, New York, September 2001. Courtesy of George W. Bush Presidential Library.

and began shouting thanks to the first responders. Someone called out, "We can't hear you." Bush shouted back through the bullhorn. "I can hear you! The rest of the world hears you! And the people who knocked these buildings down will hear all of us soon!" People in the crowd responded to his passion with a passion of their own as they chanted, "USA! USA!" Before he left, the president talked to a number of families of volunteer helpers who had disappeared into the rubble and had not been seen again. One, a woman named Arlene Howard, told him her son, policeman George Howard, had been missing for three days. She pressed her son's police badge into the president's hand and said, "Please remember him." George Bush carried the badge with him in the pocket of his suit all of his remaining days as president, as a reminder of those that America had lost on 9/11.

On Thursday, September 20, President Bush addressed a joint session of Congress in the Capitol, his voice loud and forceful. Throughout his speech, a standing and cheering audience made him pause. "Americans should not expect one battle but a lengthy campaign," he said, while telling the rest of the world, "Every nation . . . now has a decision to make. Either you are with us or you are with the terrorists." He said to the military, "The hour is coming when America will act, and you will make us proud." He said to Muslims, "We respect your faith. . . . The terrorists are traitors to their own faith." Bush made this point repeatedly because he feared for the safety of Muslims in America.

Then he outlined his plan. He demanded that the Taliban regime in Afghanistan surrender al-Qaeda leaders and their followers to the United States and close the terrorist training camps, a demand which he said was nonnegotiable. He also announced a new Cabinet-level office, the Department of Homeland Security.

He welcomed guests in the audience, among them British Prime Minister Tony Blair, Governor of New York George Pataki, Mayor of New York Rudolph Giuliani, and Lisa Beamer, whose husband had died in the Pennsylvania crash.

Ordinarily, after the president addresses a joint session, the opposing party delivers a response in which they refute whatever they disagree with. Democrats delivered no response. "America must speak with one voice and support the president," they said.

George Bush remained alert for more terrorist attacks, especially since Osama bin Laden had issued a religious edict,

President Bush is acknowledged by his proud father, former President George H. W. Bush, after delivering an address at the National Cathedral following the attacks on 9/11, Washington, DC, September 2001. Also in the row are (*left to right*) Barbara Bush, former President Bill Clinton, Senator Hillary Clinton, and Chelsea Clinton. Courtesy of George W. Bush Presidential Library.

called a fatwa, saying that the murder of Americans was "an individual duty for every Muslim who can do it in any country in which it is possible to do it." Frightening possibilities presented themselves daily in the form of more airplane crashes, biological warfare, attacks on embassies abroad, or individuals terrorizing on their own.

The new Department of Homeland Security took charge of protecting the nation. Most noticeable to the public was increased security at airports. Before 9/11, passengers could show up at the last minute without going through any kind of screening and without showing an ID. They could carry anything they wanted aboard the plane, and they could take non-passengers with them to the gate to say goodbye. That casual freedom disappeared permanently from airports.

America braced for the possibility of additional attacks, including those from chemical and biological warfare. On a trip to Asia, it was suspected for twenty-four hours that the president and his advisers had been poisoned and would soon die. Another biological threat came in the form of letters in the mail. A week after 9/11, people began opening envelopes containing a deadly bacterium in powder form that causes the disease anthrax. Senate Majority Leader Tom Daschle was one recipient of such a letter. Over a period of months, twenty-two people did contract the disease and five died. They included postal workers and a news media figure. An investigation led to a government scientist. When he was accused, the man killed himself. Further study suggested that he was the culprit, but it was never proven. The anthrax attacks disappeared, but many other forms of biological warfare were still possible.

Terrorists working on their own were discovered. A British man named Richard Reid, who had been in prison for mugging, converted to a radical form of Islam and decided to crash an American Airlines flight from Paris to Miami. In mid-flight, when he struck a match to light explosives hidden in his high-top tennis shoes, a flight attendant tried to stop him. He knocked her down and was immediately overwhelmed by passengers, who tied him up until they could land and turn him over to police.

One bit of news particularly disturbed Bush. He learned that the two 9/11 terrorists who flew planes into the World Trade Center had been allowed to come to the United States to learn how to fly at a Florida flight school.

President Bush, the former managing general partner and part owner of Major League Baseball's Texas Rangers, throws out the opening pitch of the 2001 World Series, New York, New York, October 2001. Courtesy of George W. Bush Presidential Library.

Seven weeks after 9/11, Bush looked forward to one duty. The New York Yankees invited him to Yankee Stadium to throw out the first pitch in the third game of the World Series against the Arizona Diamondbacks. He saw his appearance as a chance to lift the spirits of New Yorkers. While he was warming up before the game, two things put him under extra pressure. A Secret Service agent insisted he wear a bulky bulletproof vest under his jacket, which might throw off his pitching arm. Then Yankees shortstop Derek Jeter told him that if he threw from in front of the pitching mound, he would be booed, and if he bounced the ball, he would be booed. Now, not so confident, Bush walked to the mound, looked at the catcher, who seemed farther away than the usual sixty feet, six inches, wound up, and threw a perfect pitch. "USA! USA! USA!" the crowd screamed ecstatically. The Yankees won the game. Jenna remembered that after the pitch, he went directly to Laura, and they hugged and kissed. "My parents," she said, "are not affectionate in front of others . . . so I knew that they had both been nervous."

CHAPTER 6

AFGHANISTAN, IRAQ, AND GUANTÁNAMO BAY

Meanwhile, the Taliban in Afghanistan rejected Bush's demands to hand over al-Qaeda members. The president declared war, and a poll showed that more than half of the American people approved.

On October 7, the United States began an aerial bombardment of Taliban and al-Qaeda sites along with airdrops of humanitarian supplies for civilians. Then followed a ground invasion. By early December, the last Taliban stronghold had fallen, the Taliban leader had gone into hiding, and Osama bin Laden had fled from Afghanistan to Pakistan.

Nevertheless, the Taliban struggle refused to go away. Repeatedly, in the years since 2001, the Taliban has regrouped, fought fiercely, had been pushed back, and then charged forth again. The government within Afghanistan has fought the Taliban successfully when it has had international support but has been overwhelmed when that support has dwindled.

The focus then turned to Iraq. The world had been afraid of its president, Saddam Hussein, for a long time because of his brutality to his own people and his unwarranted attacks on neighboring countries. The United Nations (UN) had placed him under sanctions for fear he was producing chemical, biological, or nuclear weapons to aid terrorists, but when the organization sent arms inspectors to the country, Saddam was uncooperative and turned them away.

Bush's advisers suspected, but did not know for certain, whether Saddam was in contact with al-Qaeda, and they also suspected but did not know for certain whether Iraq was producing weapons of mass destruction. What they did know was that if Saddam produced weapons and then gave them to al-Qaeda to use against the United States, it would be disastrous. Traditionally, the United States had waited to be attacked before going to war, as it had with the war in Afghanistan. Now Bush began thinking of a war in Iraq as a "preemptive action"—stopping an enemy by attacking them first.

Before he did that, though, he tried to convince the UN that the group should be more forceful in getting Iraq to let it search the country for weapons. The UN listened but did not act. He had more luck persuading Congress to let him go forward. Both the House of Representatives and the Senate, by comfortable majorities, voted to authorize the president to use force against Iraq.

From October until March, the administration considered all possibilities. Finally losing patience with the inaction, George Bush, on March 17, 2003, demanded to Saddam Hussein that he resign from office and leave Iraq or face war. Saddam refused, and on March 20, the United States attacked, along with allies from Great Britain and smaller forces from several other countries. Within a month, they defeated the Iraqi military. Saddam went into hiding. In December of that year, he was found at the bottom of an eight-foot-deep hole on an isolated farm. Armed with a pistol, haggard, and disoriented, he offered no resistance. Of his thirty-five years in power, he said that he was a "just but firm ruler," but that was not the case. In October 2005, he went on trial before an Iraqi court. After nine months of testimony, he was convicted of crimes against humanity. On December 30, 2006, at age 69, he was hanged by Iraqi authorities, as was the punishment for conviction.

The occupation was more difficult, lasted longer, and was vastly more expensive than it had been positioned by the Bush administration. American troops remained in Iraq eight and a half years, roiling in the chaos created by those Iraqis who were for the Americans, those who hated the Americans, and ethnic subgroups who hated each other. Despite claims that Saddam had weapons of mass destruction, none were found after a search of hiding places throughout the country was made. Eventually, in 2011, when Barack Obama was president, U.S. forces withdrew from Iraq.

At first, the Navy held suspected terrorists captured in Afghanistan and Iraq on a ship in the Arabian Sea, but a place needed to be found where these prisoners would face trial. Trying them in the United States gave them the right by law to remain silent. Bush decided, instead, to house them where they would be treated as illegal enemy combatants under international law. Here they would face military tribunals, courts of justice that would determine their legal fate. They could be represented by lawyers and could appeal any decision, but their testimony was required, as it would not have been if they were tried within the United States under American citizen protection.

The treatment of prisoners at Guantánamo Bay has been a hotly debated issue among humanitarian groups, in Congress, throughout the nation, and even within the US Supreme Court. Critics have deplored the use of "enhanced interrogation" with these prisoners, including sleep deprivation for up to 180 hours, slapping, subjecting the prisoner to cold, and, most controversially, waterboarding. Waterboarding is an interrogation technique in which a prisoner is laid, face at a level below their legs, with a cloth covering their eyes; then water is poured over their face and into their nose and mouth, making them gag and feel as if they were drowning.

President Bush has maintained that these techniques were fair under the circumstances and that of the thousands of terrorists captured, about thirty were subjected to enhanced interrogation, and only three were waterboarded. He reminded Americans that thousands of lives have been saved because of information gained from captives under questioning—information about plots against diplomatic and military facilities abroad, against Heathrow Airport in London, and against multiple US targets.

Those opposed to the practices called it, simply, torture.

Like many presidents before him, George Bush believed that the United States has a responsibility to look out for those in need, both at home in our country and across the world. So, as a deadly disease called AIDS, which severely weakens the immune system, swept across the world, especially in Africa, he made a plan to help many victims who were unable to get medical care. In 2003, he established the President's Emergency Plan for AIDS Relief, or PEPFAR, which brought medical resources to fifteen of the poorest countries in the world where AIDS had spread quickly and much of their population was at risk. The plan was a great success. By 2023, the twentieth anniversary of its creation, PEPFAR had saved over twenty-five million lives, and over sixty-five million had received medical treatment and access to crucial testing services and medicine. The *New York Times* called PEPFAR "a golden moment when a president did the right thing and provided American leadership to rein in one of the deadliest epidemics in history."

CHAPTER 7

REELECTION AND ADDITIONAL CHALLENGES

Early in 2003, Bush began planning for the next year's presidential election. He asked Dick Cheney to run with him again as his vice president. Their opponents turned out to be Senator John Kerry from Massachusetts, who had originally voted for war in Iraq but was now opposing it, and his running mate, Senator John Edwards of North Carolina.

When Election Day, November 2, 2004, arrived, Bush and his family voted early in the morning at the fire station in Crawford, Texas. Later, Karl Rove telephoned Bush to say that he was worried about the results in the important swing state of Ohio, and George flew to Columbus for his twentieth visit to that state during the campaign. Finally, he flew on to Washington, DC. A second call from Rove just as he landed told him that the exit polls as people left their voting sites indicated he was not doing well. Bush said, "I felt like he had just punched me in the stomach."

The night was a long one, but as results came in, the news got better and better. It was not until 11:02 the next morning that John Kerry called Bush and conceded the election. By this time, President Bush was in his White House office. He called Laura, hugged his aides, congratulated Vice President Cheney, and called his parents. He had won narrowly, with 286 electoral votes to Kerry's 251 and with just over 50 percent of the popular vote. Bush ended up winning Ohio's twenty electoral votes.

Some analysts shortly afterward speculated that Bush had succeeded because a second 9/11 had not happened during his first term and because people were looking for "stability in leadership."

In 2005, Louisiana and the Gulf Coast were hit by Hurricane Katrina, the worst storm in over a century. In New Orleans, the levees broke, flooding the streets with the waters of Lake Pontchartrain and leaving behind chaos, looting, and thousands of people stranded on their rooftops or carried away by the flood. State and local government couldn't handle a catastrophe of such magnitude. They argued among themselves about who was in charge. The governor argued against Bush's desire to send federal troops to help. Bush sent them anyway. He also flew over the area and was photographed peering out of the window of *Air Force One* at the devastation below. Cries were heard across the country that he had sent the federal government where it was not wanted or that he hadn't sent it soon enough or that he was interested in helping only the white people who were suffering while ignoring the area's African American residents and that he looked out of that *Air Force One* window with curiosity, not with empathy. Bush's own feeling was that he wished he had sent help sooner, even if it wasn't wanted, and he wished that he had better communicated that his heart was broken for the suf-

President Bush greets a homeowner after
Hurricane Katrina, New Orleans, April 2006.
Courtesy of George W. Bush Presidential Library.

fering people he viewed from the airplane. He called the accusation that he was a racist "the worst moment of my presidency." Over the weeks following Katrina, he visited New Orleans thirteen times.

He found the response of other states and private citizens inspiring. Nearly every state took in evacuees. Houston, Texas, alone cared for 250,000 people who had been made homeless by the storm. To lead fundraising from individuals, President Bush appointed two former presidents,

George H. W. Bush and Bill Clinton, who set aside their former competition, worked well together, and became friends. Earlier that year, former President Bush and former President Clinton had also worked together at George W. Bush's request to raise funds for relief of victims of a tsunami in the Indian Ocean.

In addition to Hurricane Katrina, George Bush faced other challenges in his second term as president. In Congress, the midterm elections produced Democratic majorities in both the House and the Senate, making his legislative goals more difficult to achieve.

His nominations for Supreme Court judges were also noteworthy. His first nomination of John Roberts had been met with praise and acceptance, but his second one was criticized, even by some Republicans, to the point that the nominee requested her name be withdrawn.

He angered his own conservative supporters by signing legislation under which Medicare would pay for prescription drugs, which would be costly and was the biggest expansion of the program since its founding under President Lyndon Johnson in 1965.

Within his own administration, his foreign policy team became mired down in internal arguments until, finally, he replaced Secretary of Defense Donald Rumsfeld with Robert Gates, who had worked well in the past with Secretary of State Condoleezza Rice.

Iran and North Korea had nuclear programs that they were unwilling to abandon. This time Bush chose not to fight but to block—in every way he could—their ability to get money

President Bush meets with troops during a visit to Bagram Air Base, Afghanistan, March 2006. Courtesy of George W. Bush Presidential Library.

to further these programs. In this, he proved successful, and the next president, Barack Obama, continued this policy.

Laura Bush remarked that her husband's presidency was bookended by two Septembers: September 11, when the nation was devastated by forces from without, and the September of 2008, when it was threatened by collapse from within. Just before he left office, the United States faced a financial crisis in which huge companies were failing and the stock market lost 778 points in one day, its worst day in many years. If Bush bailed out the huge failing companies with government money, many smaller companies still would fail because they had no government subsidy. If he did not save the huge companies, the small businesses that relied on them would go out of business. No clearly right answer existed. He aided some companies, then didn't aid others, and the business world suffered either way. Among those he gave enormous loans to were General Motors and Chrysler.

Iraq remained a major concern as Bush ended his term. Opposition to the Iraq War grew stronger as American soldiers continued to die and an end to the war continued to appear distant. Congress appointed a panel, called the Iraq Study Group, to assess what the next steps should be. At the end of 2006, the group said the situation was "grave and deteriorating," and it recommended American withdrawal by 2008. George Bush decided on one more daring surge in American efforts before the military left the country. He ordered thirty thousand more troops into Iraq. By now, Iraq was in chaos, with much violence against its citizens, including kidnappings and beheadings, as well as efforts by al-Qaeda activists to recruit and train volunteers. Bush's plan was for the new troops to make daily life safe for the people, especially by working alongside the Iraqi military to teach them how to take on this protective role. For the first time, there was progress, and by the end of 2008, because of the surge and other factors, deaths of Americans and Iraqis in the country declined over 60 percent.

Regardless of the change, Americans had grown tired of war, and as Bush neared the end of the term, his popularity with the American people had decreased considerably. When he bid farewell to Americans as president in 2009, he said, "It has been the privilege of a lifetime to serve as your president. There have been good days and tough days. But every day I have been inspired by the greatness of our country, and uplifted by the goodness of our people."

CHAPTER 8
RETIREMENT

On the morning of January 20, 2009, President George Bush took a last walk around the back lawn of the White House. Then, bundled up against the 28-degree weather, he and Laura attended the inauguration of Barack Obama, who would become the forty-fourth president. President and Mrs. Obama hugged the Bushes goodbye. Later in the day they flew to Texas. At about six o'clock that night, George and Laura, now former president and First Lady, were greeted in 70-degree Midland by country and western entertainers and an enthusiastic crowd of thirty thousand. Bush joked that when his mother learned that his childhood home in Midland would be a museum, she said, "You better go clean your room." And then, more seriously, he said of Barack Obama, "A good man took the oath of office today, and we offer him our prayers for success."

Today they divide their time between their home in Dallas, their ranch in Crawford, Texas, and the family's summer home in Kennebunkport, Maine. Bush wrote his memoirs and oversaw the building of his presidential library and museum and the creation of the Bush Institute, which studies issues facing the country and the world, all on the campus of

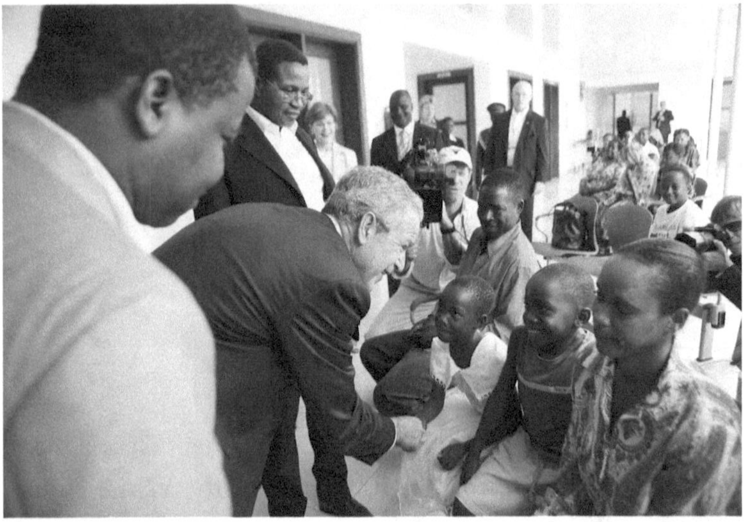

President Bush greets young AIDS patients at a hospital funded by the President's Emergency Plan for AIDS Relief (PEPFAR), which has saved over 25 million lives, Dar es Salaam, Tanzania, February 2008. Courtesy of George W. Bush Presidential Library.

SMU in Dallas. The George W. Bush Presidential Center was dedicated on a sunny April day in 2013. The hundreds of attendees from around the world included all the living presidents at the time—Jimmy Carter, George H. W. Bush, Bill Clinton, and Barack Obama—and their spouses. Each president paid tribute to Bush, commenting on his courage, his sense of humor, his love of country, and his concern for the needy of the world. Among other things, they pointed to the many lives he had saved through his PEPFAR program. Everyone said the Pledge of Allegiance and sang "America the Beautiful" and the "Battle Hymn of the Republic." An obviously happy George Bush spoke last, leaving the stage with tears in his eyes.

In the next years, he made speeches and he did extensive charitable work, especially for wounded veterans.

He watched his children grow into adults and start their own families. Jenna married into a political family; her husband, Henry Chase Hager, is the son of a former lieutenant governor of Virginia. She and her husband have three children, Mila, Poppy, and Hal. She has followed a television career as co-host of the *Today* show on NBC. Barbara, married to screenwriter Craig Coyne, has two children with her husband and is the co-founder and chair of the nonprofit Global Health Corps, which helps train young leaders for work with health systems throughout the world. Both families live in the New York area.

Bush continues to be active in his post–White House life. Upon leaving office, he already was an avid bicycler and golfer but was looking for another hobby. Reading Winston Churchill's *Painting as a Pastime* inspired him to try his own hand as a painter. He began doing portraits of famous figures from looking at photographs of them. Sometimes he worked at his painting for five or six hours a day. Becoming more serious in his intent, he got a nearby artist to come to his house for three hours every Monday morning to teach him. She called him a quick learner with a good memory.

At first he kept this pursuit of painting a secret, but, eventually, he published a book titled *Portraits of Courage*, which includes sixty-six portraits of veterans injured in Afghanistan and Iraq, and he wrote essays about each one, detailing their injuries and struggles and recovery. He had met every one of the people he painted. In 2021, he published a new book following the same format—this one about immigrants and their stories, titled *Out of Many, One*. "My hope," he says, "is that this book will help focus our collective attention on the positive impacts that immigrants are making on our country."

About his life today, Bush has remarked, "I think part of having a fulfilling life is to be challenged. I'm challenged on the golf course, I'm challenged to stay fit, and I'm challenged by my paintings. . . . I am happy."

About his presidency, he has said that he would like to be remembered as "somebody who took on tough challenges and didn't shy away from doing what he thought was right."

SELECTED BIBLIOGRAPHY

Bush, George H. W. *All the Best, George Bush: My Life in Letters and Other Writings*. Scribner, 1999.

Bush, George W. *Decision Points*. Random House, 2010.

Bush, George W. *George W. Bush: On God and Country*. Edited by Thomas Freiling. Allegiance Press, 2004.

Updegrove, Mark. *The Last Republicans: Inside the Extraordinary Relationship Between George H. W. Bush and George W. Bush*. Harper Collins, 2017.

www.ingramcontent.com/pod-product-compliance
Lightning Source LLC
LaVergne TN
LVHW100024310826
846742LV00012B/34